In The Hours Before Dawn

Poems for the Unfinished Soul

Christina Pagán

Made with ❤ on the BookLeaf Publishing Platform

www.bookleafpub.in

www.bookleafpub.com

Dedication

For my parents, whose unwavering support has been my foundation.

For my friends, who lift me with their kindness and light.

For Teapot, my quiet companion in every stolen moment of creation.

And for the girl I used to be—may she see how far we've come.

Preface

There is something sacred about the quiet moments before dawn—when the world is hushed, the mind untethered, and the heart more willing to listen. It is in these liminal hours that I have often found myself most raw, most unfinished, most real.

This collection is a meditation on transformation, longing, and the ever-evolving nature of the self. These poems are for those who are still becoming, still searching, still unraveling and weaving themselves anew. If you have ever felt caught between who you were and who you are meant to be, this book is for you.

Acknowledgements

No creation happens in isolation, and this book is no exception.

To my parents, whose steady love has been the soil in which my dreams take root. To my friends, who remind me that words are not the only way to be heard. To everyone who has ever called me an artist, even when I didn't believe it.

And to the version of me who once doubted, hesitated, waited—this is proof that we can always begin.

1. Visions

Do you see me—really see me?
Do you wish to know my mind?
Would you dare to climb my walls,
or do you fear what you might find?
There's another world inside me,
visions yet to be defined.
We can take this trip together,
if you are so inclined.

Because I want to really see you,
and I long to know your soul—
to learn all the secrets you keep hidden,
tightly under your control.
Has your brilliant heart grown weary?
Are you yearning to be whole?
To softly share your burdens
is my greatest goal.

I want to draw out your insecurities
and introduce them to my own.
I want to plant a field of daydreams
and then harvest what we've grown.
I want to dance to your heartbeat,
even when I dance alone,

as we are sublimely writing
the greatest love song ever known.

Do you see how you have touched me?
How you've lit my heart anew?
How, since the day we met,
I have known this to be true—
that you will always be a part of me,
and until this life is through,
I am grateful for every moment
that I get to spend with you.

2. Traces of Her

She was fluid like water.
Memories of her washing over you when you least
expect it.
Her inquisitive face, looking for answers no one could
give.
Her emotions ever changing like the tide.

She was wild like air.
Not able to keep up, you were just along for the ride.
Her mind racing a million miles a minute.
Her long hair tangling in the wind.

She was weathered like earth.
Hiding her truths from your watchful gaze.
Her skin taking on the colors of everything around her.
Her pain taking root like a mighty tree.

She was luminous like fire.
Glowing brighter than you could ever comprehend.
Her radiant smile belying hurts that lied buried.
Her thoughts burning with things unsaid.

But she still lingers, just beneath the surface.
Reflected in my own mirrored gaze, flickering like an

ember.

A whisper in the wind, a ripple in the tide,

The traces of her, woven into who I've become.

3. Becoming

I make myself small.
I curse my larger body for always being in the way,
for taking up more space than I think I deserve.

I stand quiet.
If I don't speak, they won't notice me.
And if they don't notice me,
they won't ask for more of me than I can give.

I start to disappear.
I can count the endless minutes until I am allowed to
leave for the day,
yet I cannot even count on one hand
the number of times I have lived for myself.

Is this all there is?
Each day an indistinguishable grain of sand
in an hourglass that measures lost opportunities,
each second a reminder of our mortality.

The roaring in my head is growing louder.
To drown it out, I spend night after night
scrolling through other people's lives,
as if our shared monotony

can be a salve to my addled soul.

It grows louder still.
The endless waves of a life unlived—
crashing, beating,
beginning to erode my sense of reality,
threatening to swallow me whole.

My eyes open.
Have I ever really seen before?
I wonder if there is one moment
that can change the whole trajectory of your life—
or is it more like an amalgam of tiny moments,
collecting like water pooling behind a dam with no
spillway,
the pressure building up
until the whole structure is undone.

I am undone.
Thoughts flood my head.
I do not know where I am going,
but I cannot stay here.
My old beliefs and patterns cling to me
like a kudzu vine—grasping ever tighter,
trying to keep me rooted.

I shake them off.

I know the pH of the soil of my soul has shifted,
no longer supporting the invasive plants of before.
A vibrant tea garden is blooming.

My body speaks.
There are no words on my lips,
but there is poetry tattooed on my soul.
Can you hear it?
It tells of mountains to climb,
treasures to unearth,
and the promise of tomorrow.

I can hear it.
It vibrates every cell of my being,
dances within me like tiny photons of sunlight
kissing the surface of a clear, blue lake.
I am noise.
I am space.
I am substance.

I am alive.

4. Echoes in Clay

Forget your past,
the long-gone relics of your youth.
They always say, *"Let bygones be bygones."*
But is it ever really that easy?

We are all reflections of who we were molded to be—
the clay barely hardened,
handprints of others still visible on our form,
small cracks emerging when we least expect them.

Does it pain you to know
that how you interact with the world
may have been shaped by others
who never knew the weight of their touch?

Does it matter
that how you were contained as a child,
how you were seen or not seen, held or not held,
can shape your sense of safety now?
Specters of disillusion rise to keep us tethered.

There is enough blame to go around,
but no single fault to be found.
The responsibility is yours, however—

to lovingly transform what you have inherited.

The artist's hands are now yours.
Take what you have been given,
and craft a design of your own making.
Shape it with the tools of learning,
tint it with the colors of connection,
glaze it with new meaning.

When they say to forget the past,
perhaps the invitation is to forge a new direction—
to go where the guiding light is so bright
that the ghosts of your youth
can no longer materialize.

And rest a while.

5. Unmooring

"I am here," I murmur to sea, to sky,
the waves counting time in breathless beats.
It's now or never. My pulse is thunder,
the unknown calling—dark yet sweet.

I stand on the shore, longing for more,
something beyond what I claim to know.
I am ready to dive, to swim, to go in—
yet daunted still by the undertow.

I was born with clouds in my eyes,
a veil of illusion drawn over my soul,
but I ache to wade into the lake of life,
to gather the fragments, to make myself whole.

I know they wait, timeless and great—,
if I could only leave the shore.
But what if this ship goes down? What if I drown
before I ever discover more?

Are you out there? Can you help me steer?
The tides are shifting, the breezes sway.
I loosen my hold, as the path unfolds—
Trusting the stars to guide my way.

6. Ruins

Have you ever felt the ground shift beneath you—
setting the stage for a form of upheaval?
The life you constructed, brick by brick,
Now standing fragile, archaic, medieval.

Did you brace against the quaking walls,
Clutching at what felt safe and known?
Or did you let the crumbling happen—
Let your old foundations be overthrown?

Change arrives unbidden, unrelenting,
A flood that shakes, winds that sweep.
It asks only this: Will you resist?
Or will you arise from your sleep?

Dare to ask why. Open the doors.
A world beyond them waits for you.
Step from the ruins into the light—
And find there what you know to be true.

7. The Language of the Abyss

Images rise, unbidden—
Faint echoes of a forgotten tongue.
They speak of what still lingers within us,
Of truths that cannot be undone.

Lost meanings surface slowly,
Like fog dissolving on a silver lake,
The quiet stirring of the beyond—
A language only the soul can wake.

Can you hear it? Are you listening?
It calls from the depths, patient and low.
Will you turn away—or dance into the dark?
And confront what it is that you know?

Listen now—let it pull you under,
In stillness, unravel, give in to its song.
For only in breaking can you become,
Only in yielding can you move on.

8. Let Freedom Ring

Meet me at the river at midnight.
The stage is set for discourse.
Our words spark, our ideas ignite,
Our presence a reckoning force.

We speak, not asking for permission.
The air is charged, resistance runs deep.
No more silence, no submission.
There is too much at stake to go back to sleep.

The atmosphere ripples with truths untold,
Whispers of a tacit dance, a wayward king,
Of loyalties bought and decencies sold.
A perversive refrain of 'let freedom ring.'

But a tide is shifting, the dawn draws near,
A beacon of hope cuts through the haze.
May our hearts stay steadfast and our vision clear,
May shadows retreat in the light that we raise.

So meet me at the river bend,
Where justice flows and resolve grows strong.
With voices united, may our chorus transcend,
Because the darker the night, the fiercer our song.

9. Invisible

What do you see when you look at me?
Or have you ever even looked at all?
I want you to know my expansive soul,
Yet I allow myself to remain small.

Your eyes seem to move through me—
past me, to prettier, shinier things.
You are searching for perfection,
not an angel with broken wings.

How could I ever be enough for you,
if you won't stop to let me in?
If all you ever see of me
is what's written in dirt upon my skin?

My heart is screaming—can you hear it?
Or has its voice worn down to dust?
Its once brilliant, untamed colors
faded now to muted rust.

I am exhausted from rejection,
my spirit growing numb.
So I turn inward to examine
the stranger I've become.

And as I glance into the mirror,
there is nothing there to see—
only the shadow of a girl
I never meant to be.

I have made myself invisible,
hidden my heart away.
No one can ever leave me
if I'm the one who doesn't stay.

How can I ask you to see me
when I refuse to meet my own eyes?
When I no longer know what is real
or what I've cleverly disguised?

I longed to be protected,
to be safe instead of afraid.
So I traded love for shelter—
but was it worth the price I've paid?

I want to open my heart again,
to set my soul free,
to unlock this cage I've created
and throw away the key.

It is not enough to ask you to love me

when I must learn to love me first.
And perhaps all I've ever needed
was already within to quench this thirst.

So I surrender my pain and fears,
allow my past to be wiped clean.
I stand before the world—unveiled, unafraid.
It is time to finally be seen.

10. All the Colors of the Rainbow

Red reminds me of the blazing sun,
right before it dips out of sight.
The streets aglow in crimson fire,
as day yields gently to night.

Orange offers memories of marigolds,
and autumn leaves dancing in the breeze.
The air, a whisper of colder days to come,
one final celebration before the freeze.

Yellow yawns of blankets of daisies in the spring,
and honeysuckle weaving through the brush.
Sunlight spilling like liquid gold,
bird songs piercing the morning hush.

Green grows visions of ancient moss,
a primordial carpet on the forest floor.
The trees stand tall, like ancient guides,
a testament to all that came before.

Blue breathes of salty ocean waves,
an endless expanse of surf and sea.
The water beckons, calling for surrender

to the swirling, cerulean symphony.

Indigo invites echoes of stormy winter skies,
deepening right before the snow.
The wind, unleashing its prescient howl,
cloaking the world in frost and shadow.

Violet vibrates with the smell of lavender,
fragrant fields under the summer sun.
A canvas brushed with dreams and whimsy,
a fleeting tapestry where daydreams run.

Memories intricately stitched together,
a masterpiece woven of time and place,
infused with the hues of joy and sorrow,
lovingly held in life's embrace.

11. Surrender

When your world feels just beyond your control,
and life's heavy burdens begin to take their toll,
surrender to the strength that's already your own.
Take a breath—trust that you're never alone.

These are the moments where we start to transform,
if we hold fast to love and ride out the storm.
Let the winds of change carry you where you're meant
to be—
and even if just for a moment, *be free*.

12. The Vortex

When the vortex hits, there is always some warning—
the subtle rising of emotions clawing toward the light,
the swell of something familiar, the bitter taste of
mourning.
And all of a sudden, you are plunged into the dark of
night.

Yet it still knocks the air right out of your chest.
Because despite how seductive it has been in the past,
you've fought your demons and sworn you've
progressed,
but you're left wondering how much longer the pain will
last.

It eclipses your happiness, leaving longing in its place.
But as dark as it can get, sweet one, you are never alone.
With all you've given to others, give yourself some
grace.
Can you not see just how much you have grown?

Why do you still feel such a need for safety and
protection?
Why do you continue to shut out your blessings from
above?

Darling, you have more than mastered the art of
introspection—
can you open up a little and allow yourself to feel this
love?

You can't spend another thirty years watching life pass
you by.
You can focus on healing, but do not put your life on
hold.
You are being called for greater things—will you heed the
cry,
or will you continue to allow your story to remain
untold?

It is time to allow this vortex to fuel your rebirth.
Transmute your pain; find a purpose for this sorrow.
My dear, your love can help to heal this earth.
So feel it all tonight—the real work begins tomorrow.

13. Dare You to Find Me

Your magazines tell me I'm not pretty enough,
that my body is the wrong size.
Your businesses say I'm not qualified,
that my intellect holds no prize.

Your social scenes whisper I lack confidence,
that I've doubted myself too long.
Your shrinks insist I feel too deeply,
that my thoughts are somehow wrong.

But if you stop—
really stop—
and look at me,
you'll see those things were never me at all.
And you will finally see what's been there all along.

I'm the girl who:

Walks alone in the woods just because she can,
never underestimating the power of nature.

Leaves handwritten notes,
believing ink on paper says more than a screen ever
could.

Holds her own in a debate,
both well-read and innately wise.

Would give you the shirt off her back,
even if only to wipe up a spill.

Loves to stand in a rainstorm,
or listen to its song upon the roof at night.

Would never lie or betray you,
because she clings to honesty and faithfulness.

Wears every color of the rainbow,
bringing light to those around her.

Sees beauty in the smallest moments,
capturing them through the lens of her soul.

Would never tear another down,
understanding the weight we all carry.

Would take on the world by your side,
just so you never have to face it alone.

But you'll never see these things in me,
not while you believe the lies you've been told.

So I urge you—
cast off society's blindfold.
And I dare you to find me.

14. Rising

There's a place that lives inside of me,
Hidden in the deep—
A place where I can simply be
And all my secrets keep.

A place where I shine bright
And you can hear me roar,
Where all my dreams take flight,
And I let my spirit soar.

Where no one tells me who I am
Or who I should become.
Where I can open up the dam
And let my waters run.

But somehow, I lost the way—
My heart is cloaked in doubt.
I need to make it back today
To let *that* woman out.

I'm surrendering to my wild spirit;
She grows stronger by the hour.
The sound is rising—can you hear it?
I introduce you to my power!

15. The Gift of Sight

I long to be seen.
Looking back, how many of my breakdowns
Were simply the weight of an unseen life?
And how many of my breakthroughs
Came from finally being recognized?

Do you long to be seen too?
I accept your doubts,
Honor your worth.
For I cannot be whole if you are fractured.

Here, in this space, you are free to explore—
The confidence that grows through connection,
The self-respect born of autonomy,
The self-esteem forged in the act of giving.

Freedom rises when we truly acknowledge one another.
And in turn, can you hold this space for others?
For we are all longing to be seen.

16. The Shape of Growth

I want to learn the art of transformation—
To study what blooms in its aftermath.
But how does one define something
As effusive yet indeterminate as evolution?

I could gather stories of struggle,
Trace the echoes of growth,
Unravel the patterns of self-reinvention
Through art and experience.

Or I could take a wider view,
Mapping the tide of collective change,
Searching for the spark—
The breath between what was and what will be.

Each account would be different.
No two journeys the same.
No two understandings in tandem.

And perhaps something is lost
In the attempt to name a thing
That lives best in the silence,
In the space where becoming is born.

17. The Breath Between

I live in the spaces on the edge,
a life punctuated by moments
neither here nor there.
No black or white—only shifting grays,
where earth dissolves into sky,
where life leans toward loss,
where becoming is never quite done.

I once feared the drift,
the weightlessness of not belonging,
but now I know—
there are dreams to be had,
wonders to weave,
in the liminality.

18. Dust or Glitter

What will remain when I am gone?
Will my deeds crumble to dust, scattered by time,
or shimmer like glitter in the hearts I've touched?

Have I carved a path that lingers,
or have I wandered too long in my own way?
Is there still time to weave a legacy,
to leave behind a light that does not fade?

Is it selfish to long for remembrance,
to hope that something of me lingers?
Even dust draws notice when it gathers,
like the weight of ordinary days.
Yet a single spark of glitter is enough
to catch the light, to be seen.

I want to be remembered for love,
for kindness that did not waver,
for the quiet strength of never giving up.
If I have touched but one soul,
does that make even dust glitter?

19. Black Willow

During an autumnal trip to Michigan, I drove through a charming town on the shores of Lake Michigan and came across a majestic black willow tree. I felt compelled to stop, spending a few quiet moments with just the tree and my camera.

A few weeks later, I searched for more information about the willow, only to discover that it had been split in two by a windstorm less than two weeks after my visit. This iconic 150-year-old tree was ultimately removed due to underlying rot.

I will forever cherish my time with this beloved willow.

I heard your ethereal call before I ever saw you,
Your sun-kissed limbs veiling your urgent demand.
I was on a path to everywhere and nowhere,
Suspended in between the sky and the land.

I saw your sparkling specter swaying in the wind;
I heeded your invitation to stop and explore.
A moment to stand under your shady halo,
A sacred space for me to rest and restore.

My hands tingled as I reached for you,
An ordinary minute of an ordinary day,
Marking a serendipitous moment in time,
Comforting me as I went on my way.

But as swiftly as you came to me,
In less than a month, you were gone,
The wind unthreading your storied limbs,
Yet your spirit lingers on.

Did you summon me, knowing your time was near,
Whispering truths only nature can see?
Or did you sense I needed your offering—
A fleeting embrace to set my heart free?

So I honor you now in words and verse,
An ephemeral wonder, a tale to be told.
For even the strongest must bow to the wind,
Yet beauty remains in the memories we hold.

20. The Magic of Living

The magic of living in found in the mundane,
The quiet of the morning, the moon's shining refrain.
The laughter that lingers, the warmth of a hand,
The courage to face what you don't understand.

It is hidden in the seconds that shimmer and fade,
It rises and falls with each promise made.
A life not just measured by the passage of time,
But the moments between, both subtle and sublime.

21. The Wait

All the "I love you"s that I speak silently in my heart
gather in the ethers,
hanging there until you remember enough to hear them
—

whether in this reality
or somewhere beyond the confines of space and time.

May you feel their echo just enough, now,
to know you are precious.
May it help carry you in times you are aching,
and may it eventually lead you home to me.